creative
casseroles

Chef
express

creative
casseroles

Published by:
TRIDENT PRESS INTERNATIONAL
801 12th Avenue South, Suite 400
Naples, Fl 34102 USA
Tel: + 1 239 649 7077
Email: tridentpress@worldnet.att.net
Websites: www.trident-international.com
           www.chefexpressinternational.com

Creative Casseroles
© Trident Press International

Publisher
Simon St. John Bailey

Editor-in-chief
Isabel Toyos

Includes Index
ISBN 1582797633
UPC 6 15269 97633 3

2004 Edition
Printed in Colombia by Cargraphics S.A.

introduction

Casserole meals are popular for three main reasons: they can be prepared ahead of time; they cook without constant attention; and they are tasty and easy to serve. Casseroles are based on a blending of the flavors of the ingredients, and most casseroles improve by being prepared in advance. Many can be fixed long before needed, and frozen

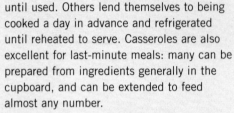

until used. Others lend themselves to being cooked a day in advance and refrigerated until reheated to serve. Casseroles are also excellent for last-minute meals: many can be prepared from ingredients generally in the cupboard, and can be extended to feed almost any number.

Casseroles are an ideal way of using leftovers; combined with other ingredients they can present a "new" meal.

Many casseroles contain all the necessary ingredients for a balanced meal –meat, vegetables and sauce– and can be served with a simple salad or crusty bread, thus relieving the cook of last-minute attention to other chores, such as cooking vegetables or preparing a salad.

Casseroles should be served in the containers in which they were cooked; with the large number of attractive ovenproof dishes now available, it should be easy to find one with the right color, shape and size for your personal preferences.

The best part of a casserole, of course, is that it cooks itself. Once all the ingredients are combined (which may be done in advance of cooking), all you have to do is relax and let it cook in the oven or on the stove while you enjoy your guests or family.

- Braising, casseroling and stewing beef are all moist methods of cookery and will tenderize less tender (and less expensive) cuts of beef. Veal, on the other hand, is already a very tender meat which is made even more tender and flavorsome by moist heat and slow cookery.

- Lamb casseroles open up a plethora of tantalizing tastes to enjoy, from Mediterranean style stews to Oriental curries and fruity casseroles.

- The flavor of pork blends well with a variety of herbs and spices, fruits and vegetables, giving a wide repertoire of tasty dishes.

- Casseroling chicken allows the extra flavors from the bone to be absorbed into the sauce and meat during cooking.

- Certain seafoods, such as octopus and squid, benefit from extended cooking times, that ensure a flavorsome, fresh and moist eating experience.

Difficulty scale

■□□ I Easy to do

■■□ I Requires attention

■■■ I Requires experience

crusty steak and kidney pie

Cooking time: 160 minutes - Preparation time: 35 minutes

method

1. Melt 30 g/1 oz butter in a saucepan over medium heat and cook meat, in batches, until brown on all sides; set aside. Add kidneys to pan and cook 1-2 minutes; set aside. Cook onion and bacon 2-3 minutes; set aside.

2. Melt remaining butter in pan over medium heat, stir in flour and cook 3-4 minutes. Gradually stir in combined sugar, stock, wine and tomato paste; stir until sauce boils and thickens. Stir in parsley and black pepper. Return meat mixture to pan, cover and simmer for 1 1/2-2 hours or until meat is tender. Cool slightly.

3. To make crust, mix butter, sour cream and egg in a bowl. Sift in 1 cup/125 g/4 oz of the flour. Add thyme and combine. Spread two-thirds of mixture over base and up the sides of a shallow ovenproof dish, then spoon in meat mixture.

4. Lightly knead remaining flour into remaining dough. Using the palm of your hand, press dough out on a lightly floured surface to 1 cm/1/2 in thick, then using a 3 cm/1 1/4 in pastry cutter, cut out rounds. Arrange rounds slightly overlapping on top of meat and bake at 180°C/350°F/Gas 4 for 30 minutes or until crust is golden.

ingredients

> 60 g/2 oz butter
> 500 g/1 lb flank skirt steak, cut into 2.5 cm/ 1 in cubes
> 3 lamb kidneys, clean and sliced
> 1 onion, chopped
> 3 rashers bacon, chopped
> 2 tablespoons flour
> 1/2 teaspoon sugar
> 3/4 cup/185 ml/6 fl oz beef stock
> 1/4 cup/60 ml/2 fl oz red wine
> 1 tablespoon tomato paste (purée)
> 1 tablespoon chopped fresh parsley
> freshly ground black pepper

sour cream crust

> 125 g/4 oz butter, softened
> 300 g/9 1/2 oz sour cream
> 1 egg
> 1 1/2 cups/185 g/6 oz self-raising flour
> 1 tablespoon chopped fresh thyme

....
Serves 4

tip from the chef

This modern version of steak and kidney pie is just as tasty as the original, but easier to make and lighter to eat.

ossobuco

■ ■ □ | Cooking time: 90 minutes - Preparation time: 20 minutes

ingredients

> **4 tablespoons olive oil**
> **1 1/2 cups pimentos, drained, cut into strips**
> **2 onions, chopped**
> **1/2 cup flour**
> **4 large veal shank slices, 4 cm/1 1/2 in thick, with the bone**
> **2 tablespoons butter**
> **1 cup dry white wine**
> **1 chicken stock cube, crushed**
> **1 1/2 cups chopped canned tomatoes**
> **1 tablespoon chopped fresh parsley**

method

1. Heat oil in a large frying pan. Add pimentos and onions and cook, stirring occasionally, until onions are translucent. Use a slotted spoon to transfer vegetables to a bowl.
2. Flour veal shanks lightly on both sides. Add butter to the frying pan; when butter foams, add veal shanks and sauté until meat is brown on all sides.
3. Add wine and cook over high heat, stirring to pick up the bits and pieces attached to the bottom of the frying pan. When wine is reduced by half, add stock cube.
4. Return vegetables to the frying pan and add tomatoes. Cover and simmer for 1 hour or until meat falls away from the bone.
5. Serve shanks in a deep dish, top with tomato sauce and garnish with parsley.

....
Serves 4

tip from the chef

This classic preparation becomes even more tasty if 3 tablespoons of diced smoked bacon are added to it.

olive
and meat ragoût

■ ■ ■ | Cooking time: 135 minutes - Preparation time: 25 minutes

method

1. Heat oil in a large saucepan over a medium heat, add beef and lamb and cook in batches until brown. Remove meat from pan and drain on absorbent kitchen paper.

2. Add onions, garlic and thyme to pan and cook, stirring, for 5 minutes or until onions are tender and golden. Return meat to pan, stir in wine, stock, tomatoes, orange rind and bouquet garni and bring to the boil. Reduce heat, cover and simmer for 1 1/2 hours or until meat is tender. Discard orange rind and bouquet garni.

3. Using a slotted spoon remove meat from pan and set aside. Bring sauce remaining in pan to the boil and boil until it reduces and thickens. Return meat to pan, add olives, parsley and black pepper to taste and cook for 20 minutes.

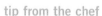

Serves 6

ingredients

> 1 tablespoon olive oil
> 500 g/1 lb chuck steak, trimmed of all visible fat and cut into 2.5 cm/1 in pieces
> 500 g/1 lb leg lamb, trimmed of all visible fat and cut into 2.5 cm/1 in pieces
> 3 onions, chopped
> 2 cloves garlic, crushed
> 1 teaspoon finely chopped fresh thyme or 1/2 teaspoon dried thyme
> 1/2 cup/125 ml/4 fl oz dry white wine
> 1 cup/250 ml/8 fl oz beef stock
> 440 g/14 oz canned tomatoes, undrained and mashed
> 5 cm/2 in piece orange rind
> bouquet garni
> 90 g/3 oz pitted black olives
> 2 tablespoons finely chopped fresh parsley
> freshly ground black pepper

tip from the chef

As with most ragoûts or stews and casseroles, this one will improve if made the day before then reheated just prior to serving.

beef with pumpkin & lemon grass

■ ■ □ | Cooking time: 110 minutes - Preparation time: 15 minutes

method

1. Heat oil in large heavy based saucepan. Cook onions over medium heat until golden. Stir in allspice, cinnamon, ginger and peppers.
2. Add meat to pan, cook over high heat until browned. Stir in lemon grass and chicken stock. Bring to the boil, reduce heat and simmer, covered, for 45 minutes.
3. Stir in pumpkin, cover and simmer for 45 minutes or until beef is tender. Remove from heat and stir in garlic. Season to taste.

....

Serves 4

ingredients

- > 2 tablespoons oil
- > 2 onions, chopped
- > 1 teaspoon whole allspice
- > 1 cinnamon stick
- > 1 teaspoon grated fresh ginger
- > 2 green peppers, sliced
- > 750 g/1 1/2 lb chuck steak, cut into 5 cm/2 in cubes
- > 2 tablespoons chopped fresh lemon grass
- > 500 ml/16 fl oz chicken stock
- > 500 g/1 lb pumpkin, cut into 4 cm/1 1/2 in cubes
- > 2 cloves garlic, crushed

tip from the chef

Serve this unusual and flavorsome dish accompanied by bowls of unflavored yogurt and topped with freshly chopped coriander.

paprika beef

■■□ | Cooking time: 100 minutes - Preparation time: 15 minutes

method

1. To make marinade, combine turmeric, paprika, chilli powder, yogurt and rind in bowl. Add steak and toss to coat. Cover and refrigerate for 2-4 hours or overnight.
2. Heat oil in large saucepan. Add onions and cook over medium heat for about 5 minutes or until onions soften. Add steak and marinade and cook over high heat for about 10 minutes or until steak is well browned.
3. Stir in wine and water. Bring to the boil, cover and simmer for about 1 1/2 hours or until steak is tender. Stir in olives and parsley, cook over medium heat for 3 minutes longer. Season to taste.

....
Serves 8

ingredients

> 1 kg/2 lb chuck steak, cut into 2 1/2 cm/1 in squares
> 4 tablespoons oil
> 2 onions, sliced
> 125 ml/4 fl oz dry white wine
> 250 ml/8 fl oz water
> 185 g/6 oz stuffed olives
> 4 tablespoons chopped fresh parsley

marinade

> 1 teaspoon ground turmeric
> 1 1/2 tablespoons mild paprika
> 1/2 teaspoon chilli powder
> 220 g/7 oz plain natural yogurt
> 2 teaspoons grated lemon rind

tip from the chef

Chunks of beef are marinated and then cooked in a flavorsome liquid. Remember, the longer your meat is in the marinade, the more tasty and tender it will be.

beef
and red wine casserole

■□□ I Cooking time: 170 minutes - Preparation time: 15 minutes

ingredients

> **4 tablespoons olive oil**
> **3/4 cup chopped bacon, rind removed**
> **1 large onion, chopped**
> **750 g/1 1/2 lb blade steak, fat removed, cut into 2 cm/3/4 in cubes**
> **2 tablespoons tomato paste (purée)**
> **2 cloves garlic, crushed**
> **1 cup red wine**
> **1/4 cup brandy**
> **1 cup beef stock**
> **1 tablespoon grated orange rind**
> **1/4 cup chopped spring onions**
> **orange rind for garnish**

method

1. Heat oil in a large frying pan over moderate heat. Add bacon and onion, cook for 2 minutes. Increase heat to high and add meat, brown rapidly on all sides, then add tomato paste and garlic.
2. Add wine, brandy, stock and orange rind, cover and cook for a further 15 minutes.
3. Transfer to a large ovenproof dish, cover and cook in a moderately low oven for 2 1/2 hours.
4. Sprinkle spring onions on top when serving, and garnish with orange rind if desired.

....

Serves 6

tip from the chef

Add 1 sliced carrot, 1/2 sliced red pepper and 1 cubed potato to this delicious casserole, if desired.

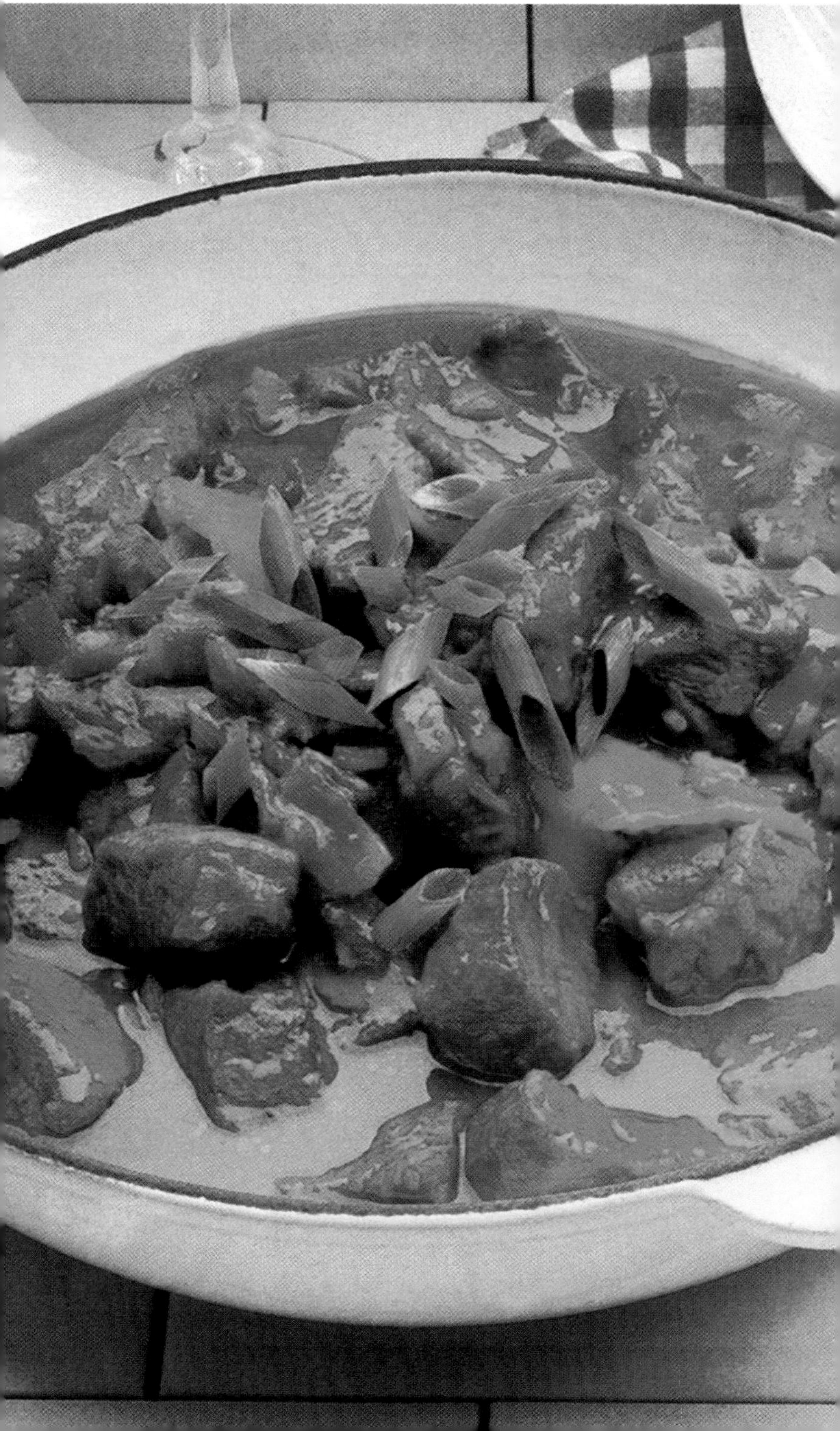

seasoned
sausage ragoût

a

■ ■ □ I Cooking time: 30 minutes - Preparation time: 25 minutes

method

1. Combine ground veal, parsley, basil, nuts, oil, garlic, pepper, breadcrumbs and cheese in large bowl (a), mix until well combined. Shape into 12 sausages (b), 10 cm/4 in long. Roll in seasoned flour.

2. Heat oil in deep frying pan. Cook sausages a few at a time (c) until browned but not cooked through. Remove sausages and drain on absorbent kitchen paper. Repeat with remaining sausages.

3. Arrange sausages, potatoes and onions in deep saucepan. Combine soy sauce, juice, stock, wine and basil in bowl, pour into saucepan (d). Bring to the boil, reduce heat and simmer, covered, for 20 minutes or until potatoes are tender. Thicken sauce in pan, if desired.

....

Serves 6

tip from the chef

For a complete meal, serve this tasty ragoût with a chilled tomato salad and crusty French bread.

ingredients

> 500 g/1 lb ground veal
> 60 g/2 oz finely chopped fresh parsley
> 60 g/2 oz finely chopped fresh basil
> 3 tablespoons pine nuts
> 1 tablespoon olive oil
> 2 cloves garlic, crushed
> 1 teaspoon cracked black peppercorns
> 185 g/6 oz fresh breadcrumbs
> 60 g/2 oz grated fresh Parmesan cheese
> seasoned flour
> oil for deep frying
> 3 tablespoons soy sauce
> 125 ml/4 fl oz lemon juice
> 250 ml/8 fl oz chicken stock
> 250 ml/8 fl oz dry white wine
> 12 whole baby potatoes, scrubbed
> 12 whole baby onions
> 3 tablespoons chopped fresh basil

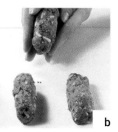

b

c

d

chunky
lamb soup

■ ■ □ | Cooking time: 100 minutes - Preparation time: 15 minutes

ingredients

> 2 tablespoons butter
> 500 g/1 lb lamb fillet, cut into 2 cm/³/4 in cubes
> 1 large onion, chopped
> 1 tablespoon chopped fresh parsley
> 2 teaspoons paprika
> 1 teaspoon saffron powder
> 1 teaspoon cracked black peppercorns
> 6 cups chicken stock
> ¹/3 cup chickpeas, soaked overnight, drained
> 2 cups peeled tomatoes, seeded and chopped
> ¹/4 cup lemon juice
> ¹/4 cup rice

method

1. Melt butter in a large saucepan over a medium heat. Add lamb pieces, onion, parsley, paprika, saffron and pepper, cook for 5 minutes, stirring frequently.

2. Add stock, chickpeas, tomatoes and lemon juice. Cover saucepan and simmer gently for 1¹/4 hours.

3. Add rice and cook for a further 20 minutes or until rice is tender; serve immediately.

....

Serves 6

tip from the chef

Shredded peppers, leeks and carrots can be added to this delicious soup.

lamb stew
with lemon sauce

■ ■ □ I Cooking time: 100 minutes - Preparation time: 15 minutes

method

1. Slice lamb into 2 cm/³/₄ in cubes, discarding any fat. Place lamb into a large saucepan with onion, pepper and celery. Add enough stock to just cover meat, approximately 2¹/₂ cups.

2. Bring to the boil and skim until the surface is clear. Cover and simmer for 1-1¹/₂ hours until meat is tender.

3. Transfer meat and vegetables to a deep serving dish, using a slotted spoon. Keep meat warm in a low oven. Strain stock and reserve 1¹/₂ cups.

4. Melt butter in a medium saucepan. Add flour and stir over moderate heat for 2 minutes. Pour in reserved stock, stir until mixture is smooth and slightly thickened, about 3 minutes.

5. Beat egg yolks with lemon juice with a whisk. Pour ¹/₄ cup of hot stock mixture into egg lemon mixture, whisk until smooth. Pour this mixture into stock and stir constantly over a low heat until sauce thickens; do not boil. Pour sauce over meat and serve immediately. Garnish with fresh dill if desired.

ingredients

> **1 shoulder of lamb, boned**
> **2 medium onions, chopped**
> **1 red pepper, seeded and chopped**
> **2 sticks celery, sliced**
> **2¹/₂ cups chicken stock**
> **40 g/1¹/₂ oz butter**
> **2 tablespoons plain flour**
> **2 egg yolks**
> **¹/₄ cup lemon juice**
> **sprig of dill, for garnish**

....
Serves 6

tip from the chef
The sauce should not boil, as it would curdle. If it does, blend it for some seconds.

lamb pot roast

■■□ | Cooking time: 90 minutes - Preparation time: 15 minutes

ingredients

- > **90 g/3 oz butter**
- > **1.5-2 kg/3-4 lb leg of lamb**
- > **1 teaspoon sugar**
- > **1/4 teaspoon mixed dried herbs**
- > **440 g/14 oz canned tomatoes, undrained and mashed**
- > **1/2 cup/125 ml/4 fl oz red wine**
- > **2 tablespoons tomato paste (purée)**
- > **1 tablespoon Worcestershire sauce**
- > **freshly ground black pepper**
- > **2 tablespoons vegetable oil**
- > **3 carrots, halved lengthwise**
- > **3 turnips, halved lengthwise**
- > **3 large potatoes, halved**
- > **6 small onions**

method

1. Melt 30 g/1 oz butter in a heavy-based frying pan over a medium heat and cook meat until brown on all sides (a). Combine sugar, herbs, tomatoes, wine, tomato paste (purée), Worcestershire sauce and black pepper to taste and pour over meat (b). Bring to the boil, then reduce heat, cover and simmer for 1 1/2 hours or until meat is tender.

2. About 30 minutes before meat finishes cooking, heat oil and remaining butter in a heavy-based frying pan over a medium heat, add carrots, turnips, potatoes and onions and cook until lightly browned. Reduce heat to low, cover and cook for 15-20 minutes or until vegetables are tender.

3. Transfer vegetables to meat pan (c). Boil for 10 minutes or until sauce reduces and thickens slightly. Serve sauce with meat and vegetables.

....

Serves 6

tip from the chef

Pot roasting dates back to prehistoric times when clay pots were filled with game, whole cuts of meat or poultry and vegetables, then hung over a fire to simmer. Lean meats that need long slow cooking are ideal for pot roasting. A nut of veal, a whole chicken or a piece of topside beef are also delicious cooked in this way.

a   b   c

athenian
lamb hotpot

■ ■ □ | Cooking time: 100 minutes - Preparation time: 15 minutes

method

1. Trim meat of all visible fat. Heat 2 tablespoons of oil in a large saucepan. Cook the meat in batches until well browned on all sides. Transfer to a plate and set aside.

2. Heat remaining oil and cook onion and pepper for 2-3 minutes or until onion softens. Stir in tomato paste and stock. Stir well to lift pan sediment.

3. Add cardamom, cinnamon and pepper. Bring to the boil, reduce heat and simmer for 5 minutes. Return meat to the pan with coriander. Cover and simmer for 1¹/₂ hours or until meat is tender and sauce thickens.

....
Serves 6

ingredients

> 1 kg/2 lb boneless lamb, cubed
> 3 tablespoons olive oil
> 2 onions, finely chopped
> 1 green pepper, seeded and chopped
> 250 ml/8 fl oz tomato paste
> 185 ml/6 fl oz chicken stock
> ¹/₂ teaspoon ground cardamom
> 1 large cinnamon stick
> freshly ground black pepper
> 2 tablespoons chopped fresh coriander

tip from the chef

Shiraz wine, with its spiced touch, goes great with lamb.

garlicky lamb pot roast

■ ■ ■ | Cooking time: 70 minutes - Preparation time: 25 minutes

method

1. Combine garlic, garam masala, breadcrumbs, pine nuts, currants and rind in a glass bowl. Spoon mixture into lamb cavity and secure with string. Combine nutmeg, cinnamon and pepper, rub over all surfaces of lamb.

2. Heat oil in large saucepan. Add meat and cook over high heat until browned. Add stock, cover and simmer over low heat for 25 minutes, turning occasionally. Mix in lemon juice, cover and simmer for 25 minutes longer. Add kumara and simmer for 5 minutes more. Remove lamb from pan and set aside and keep warm. Add beans and cook until tender. Season to taste. To serve, slice lamb and accompany with vegetables.

....
Serves 8

ingredients

> 3 cloves garlic, crushed
> 1 teaspoon garam masala
> 125 g/4 oz fresh breadcrumbs
> 2 tablespoons pine nuts
> 1 tablespoon currants
> 1 teaspoon grated lemon rind
> 1 1/2 kg/3 lb leg lamb, tunnel boned
> 1/2 teaspoon ground nutmeg
> 1/2 teaspoon ground cinnamon
> 1/2 teaspoon ground black pepper
> 2 tablespoons olive oil
> 2 cups chicken stock
> 2 tablespoons lemon juice
> 250 g/8 oz kumara (orange sweet potato), cut into julienne
> 250 g/8 oz green beans, topped and tailed

tip from the chef

Kumara or kumera is the name for an orange-colored sweet potato in several countries, such as Australia and New Zealand.

tomato
and thyme shanks

■ ■ □ | Cooking time: 150 minutes - Preparation time: 10 minutes

method

1. Place shanks, shallots and red pepper in a large casserole dish. Combine tomato sauce, vinegar, water, garlic and thyme and pour over shanks.
2. Cover and bake at 150°C/300°F/Gas2 for 2¹/₂ hours or until meat is very tender. Season to taste with pepper. Serve immediately or allow to cool and serve at room temperature.

....
Serves 4

ingredients

> **4 lamb shanks**
> **2 shallots, chopped**
> **1 red pepper, chopped**
> **250 ml/8 fl oz tomato sauce**
> **125 ml/4 fl oz cider vinegar**
> **250 ml/8 fl oz water**
> **1 clove garlic, crushed**
> **1 teaspoon finely chopped fresh thyme**
> **freshly ground black pepper**

tip from the chef

Served either hot or cold, these lamb shanks are a delicious and filling family meal. When cooked, the meat should be very tender and almost falling off the bone.

tarragon pork with vegetables

■■□ | Cooking time: 60 minutes - Preparation time: 20 minutes

ingredients

> **2 tablespoons butter**
> **1 kg/2 lb boned and rolled shoulder of pork**
> **2 onions, chopped**
> **1 leek, chopped**
> **750 ml/1¼ pt chicken stock**
> **3 tablespoons lemon juice**
> **1 teaspoon cracked black pepper**
> **2 dried bay leaves**
> **1 turnip, chopped**
> **12 baby potatoes, washed and drained**
> **2 carrots, chopped**
> **2 sticks celery, chopped**
> **3 tablespoons redcurrant jelly**
> **2 tablespoons chopped fresh tarragon**

method

1. Heat butter in large saucepan. Add pork and cook over high heat until browned on all sides. Add onions and leek to pan with meat and cook over low heat for 5 minutes or until onion softens.
2. Add stock, lemon juice, pepper and bay leaves, bring to the boil. Reduce heat and simmer, covered, for 30 minutes, turning meat occasionally. Add turnip, potatoes, carrots and celery and simmer, covered, for 15 minutes longer or until vegetables are firm but tender and meat is cooked through.
3. Remove meat and vegetables from pan. Set aside and keep warm. Bring pan juices to the boil and boil, uncovered, for 2 minutes. Stir in redcurrant jelly and tarragon and simmer for 5 minutes. To serve, slice pork, accompany with vegetables and spoon over sauce.

....
Serves 6

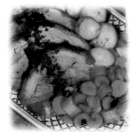

tip from the chef

A succulent pot roast of pork with vegetables delicately flavored with fresh tarragon.

mustard
chilli pork

a

■■□ | Cooking time: 50 minutes - Preparation time: 15 minutes

method

1. Trim meat of all visible fat, brush with melted butter (a) and bake at 180°C/350°F/Gas 4 for 25-30 minutes.
2. Heat ghee and oil in a saucepan, cook onions, mustard seeds, garlic and chilies for 2-3 minutes or until onions soften.
3. Stir in cumin, turmeric, brown sugar, water, lime juice and lime leaves. Bring to the boil, then reduce heat and simmer, uncovered, for 10 minutes or until mixture reduces and thickens (b).
4. Transfer mixture to a food processor or blender. Process until smooth (c), then return to pan. Slice pork diagonally (d) and add to mustard mixture. Heat through gently and serve.

ingredients

> **750 g/1¹/2 lb pork fillets**
> **60 g/2 oz melted butter**
> **30 g/1 oz ghee**
> **2 tablespoons peanut oil**
> **3 onions, chopped**
> **1 tablespoon black mustard seeds**
> **2 cloves garlic, crushed**
> **2 red chilies, chopped**
> **¹/2 teaspoon ground cumin**
> **¹/2 teaspoon ground turmeric**
> **1 tablespoon brown sugar**
> **250 ml/8 fl oz water**
> **1 tablespoon lime juice**
> **8 kasmir lime leaves**

....
Serves 4

tip from the chef

Perfect pork transformed into an exciting dish for a special occasion. The fiery taste of mustard and chilli is a wonderful complement to the zesty tang of lime.

b

c

d

chicken chasseur

■■□ | Cooking time: 100 minutes - Preparation time: 15 minutes

ingredients

> **1 tablespoon olive oil**
> **1.5 kg/3 lb chicken pieces**
> **1/2 cup/125 ml/4 fl oz dry white wine**
> **2 cups/500 ml/16 fl oz chicken stock**
> **3 tablespoons tomato paste (purée)**
> **2 tablespoons brandy**
> **1 tablespoon chopped fresh parsley**
> **1 tablespoon chopped fresh tarragon**
> **125 g/4 oz mushrooms, sliced**
> **freshly ground black pepper**

method

1. Heat oil in a large saucepan over a medium heat and cook chicken in batches, turning frequently, for 10 minutes or until brown on all sides. Remove chicken from pan and drain on absorbent kitchen paper.
2. Stir wine, stock, tomato paste (purée), brandy, parsley and tarragon into pan and bring to the boil. Return chicken to pan, reduce heat, cover and simmer, stirring occasionally, for 1 hour.
3. Add mushrooms to pan and cook for 20 minutes longer or until chicken is tender. Season to taste with black pepper.

....

Serves 6

tip from the chef

Chasseur denotes a sautéed dish with a sauce made from mushrooms, tomatoes and white wine.

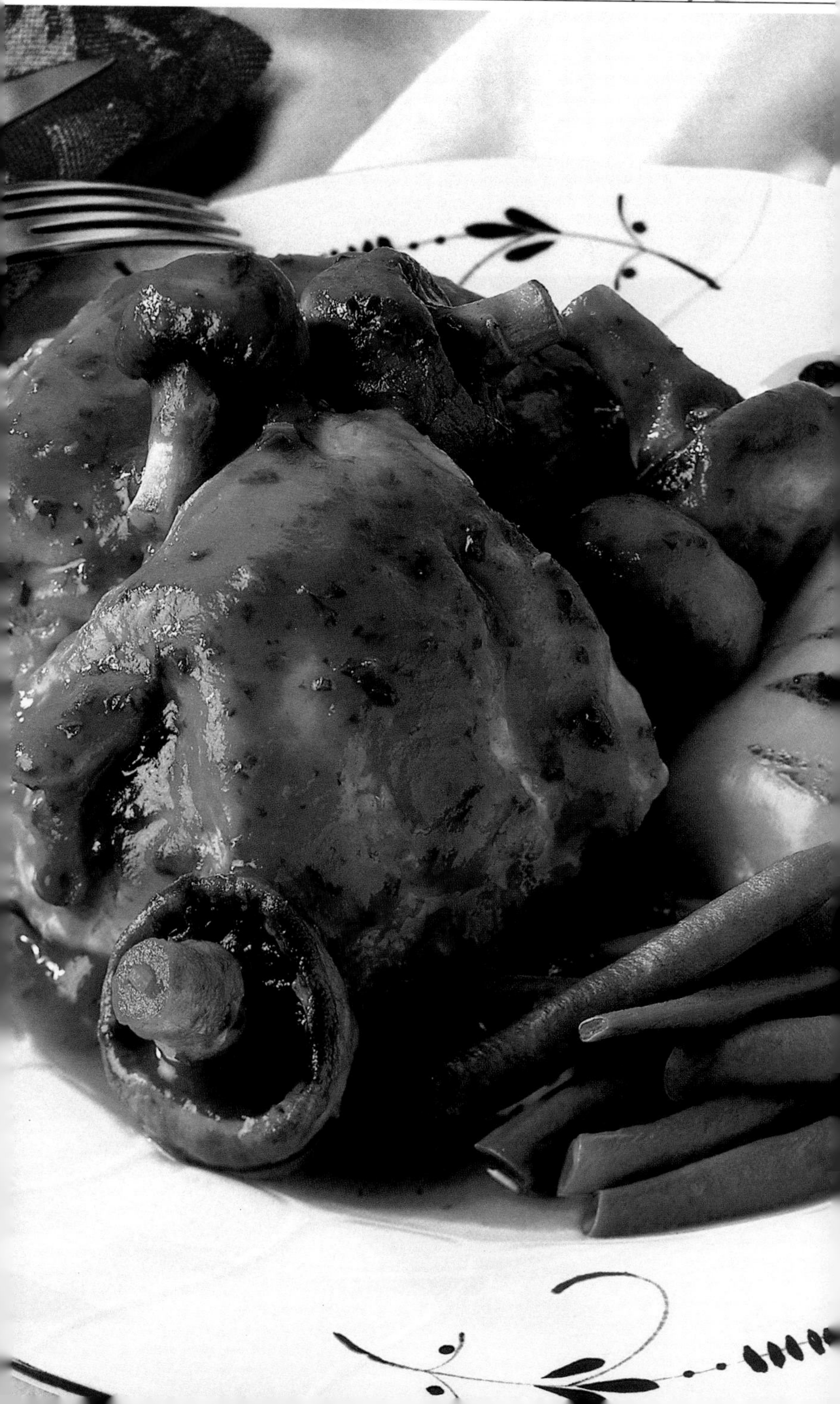

chicken cassoulet

■ ■ □ | Cooking time: 100 minutes - Preparation time: 20 minutes

method

1. Place beans in a large bowl, cover with water and set aside to soak overnight, then drain. Place beans in a large saucepan with enough water to cover and bring to the boil. Boil for 10 minutes, then reduce heat and simmer for 1 hour or until beans are tender. Drain and set aside.

2. Heat oil in a large saucepan over a medium heat, add chicken and cook, stirring, for 10 minutes or until chicken is brown on all sides. Remove from pan and drain on absorbent kitchen paper.

3. Add garlic, onions and leeks to pan and cook, stirring, for 5 minutes or until onions are golden. Add salami, tomatoes, wine and bouquet garni and bring to the boil. Reduce heat and simmer for 10 minutes. Return chicken to pan, cover and simmer for 30 minutes or until chicken is tender. Season to taste with black pepper.

4. Spoon half the chicken mixture into a large casserole dish and top with half the beans. Repeat with remaining chicken mixture and beans to use all ingredients. Sprinkle with breadcrumbs and bake at 200°C/400°F/ Gas 6, uncovered, for 30 minutes or until hot and bubbling and top is golden.

Serves 6

ingredients

> **750 g/1 1/2 lb dried haricot or borlotti beans**
> **2 tablespoons olive oil**
> **1 kg/2 lb chicken thigh or breast fillets, cut into 2 cm/3/4 in cubes**
> **2 cloves garlic, thinly sliced**
> **2 onions, chopped**
> **2 leeks, sliced**
> **250 g/8 oz salami, chopped**
> **2 x 440 g/14 oz canned tomatoes, undrained and mashed**
> **1/2 cup/125 ml/4 fl oz dry white wine**
> **1 bouquet garni**
> **freshly ground black pepper**
> **2 cups/125 g/4 oz wholemeal breadcrumbs, made from stale bread**

tip from the chef

Beans are an essential ingredient for any cassoulet as they give the dish its characteristic creaminess and flavor. For a quicker version of this dish canned beans can be used.

chicken
with chickpeas

■ ■ □ | Cooking time: 70 minutes - Preparation time: 15 minutes

ingredients

> ¹/4 cup olive oil
> 1 onion, chopped
> 1 teaspoon turmeric
> 1 chicken, cut into
  6 pieces
> 225 g/7 oz chickpeas,
  soaked overnight, drained
> 2 cups chicken stock
> ¹/4 cup lemon juice
> 3 cloves garlic, crushed
> 2 tablespoons blanched
  almonds
> 1 tablespoon chopped
  fresh parsley

method

1. Heat oil in a large frying pan, add onion and turmeric, fry for 3 minutes. Add chicken pieces and cook slowly in oil, turning it over until golden all over.

2. Add chickpeas and enough stock to cover. Stir in lemon juice and garlic, bring to the boil, reduce heat and simmer for 1 hour or until chicken is very tender.

3. Just before serving, brown almonds in the oven. Arrange chickpea mixture in the bottom of a serving dish, place chicken pieces on top and garnish with almonds and parsley.

Serves 4

tip from the chef

Almonds give an elegant touch to this original recipe. Roasting them enhances their flavor.

farmhouse
casserole

■■□ | Cooking time: 90 minutes - Preparation time: 20 minutes

method

1. Toss chicken in flour to coat. Shake off excess flour and reserve 1 tablespoon.
2. Melt butter in a frying pan over a medium heat and cook chicken, in batches, until brown. Place in a casserole dish.
3. Add garlic and reserved flour to pan and cook over a low heat, stirring, for 1 minute. Combine stock and tomato paste (purée). Remove pan from heat, stir in stock mixture, return to heat and cook over a medium heat, stirring constantly, until mixture boils and thickens. Pour mixture over chicken, cover and bake at 200°C/400°F/Gas 6 for 30 minutes.
4. Heat oil in a frying pan over a medium heat, add carrots, turnip and parsnip and cook for 3-4 minutes. Remove from pan and set aside. Add onions and bacon to pan and cook for 4-5 minutes or until bacon is crisp. Add turnip and onion mixtures, potatoes, parsley and black pepper to taste to chicken mixture and bake for 40 minutes or until vegetables are tender.

ingredients

> **1.5 kg/3 lb chicken pieces**
> **¼ cup/30 g/1 oz seasoned flour**
> **60 g/2 oz butter**
> **2 cloves garlic, crushed**
> **2½ cups/600 ml/1 pt chicken stock**
> **2 tablespoons tomato paste (purée)**
> **1 tablespoon vegetable oil**
> **2 small carrots, diced**
> **1 turnip, diced**
> **1 parsnip, diced**
> **8 small onions**
> **3 rashers bacon, chopped**
> **8 baby potatoes, quartered**
> **3 tablespoons chopped fresh parsley**
> **freshly ground black pepper**

....
Serves 4

tip from the chef

For an exotic flavor twist, add 1 tablespoon curry powder or curry paste to the pan with garlic at the beginning of step 3.

fruity chicken casserole

■■□ | Cooking time: 40 minutes - Preparation time: 15 minutes

method

1. Lightly coat chicken with flour. Heat oil in large saucepan, add chicken pieces and cook over medium heat for 8 minutes or until golden brown. Remove from pan and drain on absorbent kitchen paper.

2. Add onions and potatoes to pan, cook over low heat for about 5 minutes or until onion softens. Stir in stock, juices and honey. Return chicken to pan, add apricots, apples and prunes. Bring mixture to the boil and simmer, covered, for 20 minutes or until chicken and fruits are tender.

3. Just before serving, stir in olives and thyme. Season to taste.

....
Serves 6

ingredients

> **12 chicken wings, rinsed and drained**
> **3 tablespoons oil**
> **3 tablespoons plain flour**
> **2 onions, sliced**
> **12 baby potatoes, scrubbed**
> **250 ml/8 fl oz chicken stock**
> **250 ml/8 fl oz apple juice or cider**
> **125 ml/4 fl oz lemon juice**
> **125 ml/4 fl oz honey**
> **220 g/7 oz whole dried apricots**
> **220 g/7 oz dried apples, chopped**
> **90 g/3 oz prunes, pitted**
> **12 black olives**
> **1 tablespoon chopped fresh lemon thyme**

tip from the chef
This Middle Eastern inspired casserole looks great served on a bed of saffron rice and garnished with fresh thyme sprigs.

creamy chicken with sweet potato

a

■ ■ □ | Cooking time: 50 minutes - Preparation time: 20 minutes

method

1. Heat oil in large saucepan. Toss chicken pieces in flour (a). Add to pan and cook over medium heat until browned (b). Remove from pan and drain on absorbent paper. Set aside and keep warm.

2. Add onions to pan, cook over low heat for 5 minutes or until soft. Stir in curry powder and mustard seeds, cook for 2 minutes stirring continually. Stir in tomatoes, wine (c) and chicken stock, bring to boil, then reduce heat.

3. Return chicken to saucepan and add sweet potato. Simmer, covered, for about 30 minutes or until chicken is cooked and potato is tender. Combine garlic, basil, mayonnaise and sour cream in small bowl. Add to saucepan (d), stirring over low heat until just warmed through. Season to taste.

....
Serves 4

ingredients

> 3 tablespoons oil
> 8 chicken thighs
> 3 tablespoons plain flour
> 2 onions, sliced
> 1 tablespoon mild curry powder
> 1 teaspoon brown mustard seeds
> 250 ml/8 fl oz dry white wine
> 250 ml/8 fl oz chicken stock
> 440 g/14 oz canned tomatoes, chopped
> 500 g/1 lb sweet potato, cut into 2.5 cm/1 in cubes
> 2 cloves garlic, crushed
> 3 tablespoons finely chopped fresh basil
> 2 tablespoons mayonnaise
> 2 tablespoons sour cream

tip from the chef

The combination of chicken and sweet potato with a hint of curry makes a delicious family meal.

b

c

d

chicken biryani

■ ■ □ | Cooking time: 50 minutes - Preparation time: 20 minutes

method

1. Heat ghee in a large frying pan, cook onions for 2-3 minutes, remove and set aside. Add chicken to pan, cook until browned on all sides, remove and set aside.

2. Combine garlic and spices, stir into pan and cook for 1-2 minutes. Add stock, yogurt and cream, stirring to lift pan sediment. Return chicken to pan with half the onions. Cover and simmer for 15-20 minutes. Remove from heat and stand, covered, for 15 minutes.

3. To make rice pilau, heat ghee in a large saucepan. Cook spices, salt and rice for 1-2 minutes. Pour in stock, bring to the boil. Add sultanas, reduce heat and cook for 10-15 minutes or until most of the stock is absorbed. Cover and set aside for 10 minutes.

4. Transfer half the rice to a large ovenproof dish, top with chicken pieces, then remaining rice. Drizzle over sauce from chicken, top with remaining onions and cashew nuts. Cover and bake at 180°C/350°F/Gas 4 for 20-30 minutes.

Serves 4

ingredients

- > **3 tablespoons ghee**
- > **3 onions, sliced**
- > **1¹/₂ kg/3 lb chicken pieces**
- > **3 cloves garlic, crushed**
- > **2 teaspoons grated fresh ginger**
- > **¹/₂ teaspoon each ground cumin and cinnamon**
- > **¹/₄ teaspoon each ground cloves, cardamom and nutmeg**
- > **250 ml/8 fl oz chicken stock**
- > **125 g/4 oz unflavored yogurt**
- > **125 ml/4 fl oz cream**

rice pilau

- > **2 tablespoons ghee**
- > **¹/₂ teaspoon each ground saffron and cardamom**
- > **1 teaspoon salt**
- > **210 g/6¹/₂ oz basmati rice, well washed**
- > **1 liter/1³/₄ pt chicken stock**
- > **2 tablespoons sultanas**
- > **60 g/2 oz chopped hew nuts, roasted**

tip from the chef

The great Mogul emperors served biryani at lavish feasts on plates so large that two people were required to carry them.

duck
with ratatouille

■ ■ □ I Cooking time: 70 minutes - Preparation time: 15 minutes

ingredients

- > **1 tablespoon olive oil**
- > **1.5 kg/3 lb duck, cut into pieces**
- > **2 cloves garlic, crushed**
- > **1 large onion, cut into wedges**
- > **1 large red pepper, chopped**
- > **1 large green pepper, chopped**
- > **125 g/4 oz button mushrooms, halved**
- > **440 g/14 oz canned tomatoes, undrained and mashed**
- > **100 g/3¹/2 oz dried figs**
- > **3 sprigs fresh thyme or 1 teaspoon dried thyme**
- > **2 tablespoons chopped fresh basil or 1 teaspoon dried basil**
- > **2 cups/500 ml/16 fl oz chicken stock**
- > **¹/4 cup/60 ml/2 fl oz red wine**

method

1. Heat oil in a large saucepan over a medium heat, add duck and cook, turning frequently, for 10 minutes or until brown on all sides. Remove duck from pan and drain on absorbent kitchen paper.

2. Add garlic and onion to pan and cook, stirring, for 3 minutes or until onion is golden. Add red pepper, green pepper and mushrooms and cook for 5 minutes longer. Stir tomatoes, figs, thyme, basil, stock and wine into pan and bring to the boil. Reduce heat and simmer for 10 minutes.

3. Return duck to pan, cover and cook over a medium heat for 40 minutes or until duck is tender.

....

Serves 4

tip from the chef

For a complete meal serve this tasty duck dish with wild rice pilau or potato and cheese pancake.

marinated
rabbit hotpot

■ ■ □ | Cooking time: 95 minutes - Preparation time: 20 minutes

method

1. To make marinade, place all ingredients except wine in a glass bowl. Add rabbit, then pour over enough red wine to cover. Cover and marinate in the refrigerator overnight. Remove rabbit, strain marinade into a clean bowl and reserve. Discard solids.

2. Heat 2 tablespoons oil in a flameproof baking dish. Add rabbit and bake at 180°C/350°F/Gas 4 for 20-25 minutes or until lightly brown. Remove rabbit from dish and keep warm. Place dish with pan juices over a high heat, add onions and bacon and cook for 4-5 minutes or until golden. Set aside.

3. Melt remaining oil in dish over a medium heat, stir in flour and stir until dark brown. Gradually stir in 3 cups/750 ml/1 1/4 pt of the reserved marinade and stock. Stir constantly until sauce boils and thickens.

4. Whisk in mustard and tomato paste. Return rabbit and onion mixture to dish, cover and bake 30 minutes. Stir in remaining ingredients, cover and bake for 30 minutes longer.

....

Serves 6

ingredients

> 3 x 1 kg/2 lb rabbits, each cut into 4 portions
> 4 tablespoons olive oil
> 12 baby onions
> 6 rashers bacon, chopped
> 1/4 cup/30 g/1 oz flour
> 3 cups/750 ml/1 1/4 pt chicken stock
> 2 tablespoons French mustard
> 3 tablespoons tomato paste (purée)
> 440 g/14 oz canned butter beans, rinsed and drained
> 250 g/8 oz button mushrooms
> freshly ground black pepper

red wine marinade

> 1 onion, 1 carrot and 2 stalks celery, sliced
> 3 bay leaves
> 2 cloves garlic, crushed
> 1 tablespoon each chopped fresh tarragon and parsley
> 4 whole cloves
> 1/2 cup/125 ml/4 fl oz olive oil
> red wine

tip from the chef

Rabbit is very lean, making this robust winter dish a good idea for those who need to reduce cholesterol in their diets.

baby octopus in red wine

■ ■ □ | Cooking time: 110 minutes - Preparation time: 20 minutes

method

1. Remove tentacles, intestines and ink sac from octopus. Cut out the eyes and beak. Remove skin and rinse well.
2. Place octopus in a large saucepan, cover and simmer for 15 minutes. Drain off any juices and set aside to cool slightly.
3. Heat oil in a saucepan and cook shallots for 2-3 minutes. Add garlic and octopus and cook for 4-5 minutes. Pour wine into pan and cook over medium heat, until almost all the wine has evaporated.
4. Combine stock, tomatoes, lemon rind, pepper and coriander. Cover and simmer gently for 1 1/2 hours until octopus is tender.

Serves 6

ingredients

> 1 kg/2 lb baby octopus
> 3 tablespoons oil
> 6 shallots, chopped
> 2 cloves garlic, crushed
> 125 ml/4 fl oz dry red wine
> 125 ml/4 fl oz chicken stock
> 440 g/14 oz canned tomatoes, undrained and mashed
> 1 teaspoon grated lemon rind
> freshly ground black pepper
> 2 tablespoons finely chopped coriander

tip from the chef

Boiled potatoes sprinkled with paprika make a perfect side dish for this delicious stew.

broccoli
and macaroni casserole

■ ■ □ | Cooking time: 45 minutes - Preparation time: 15 minutes

ingredients

> 250 g/8 oz macaroni
> 500 g/1 lb broccoli, cut into florets
> 2 tablespoons olive oil
> 1 onion, finely diced
> 2 cloves garlic, crushed
> 1 tablespoon finely chopped fresh basil or 1 teaspoon dried basil
> 155 g/5 oz tasty cheese (mature Cheddar), grated
> 60 g/2 oz grated Parmesan cheese
> 250 g/8 oz cottage cheese, drained
> 2 tablespoons milk
> freshly ground black pepper

method

1. Cook pasta in boiling water in a large saucepan following packet directions. Drain, set aside and keep warm.
2. Boil, steam or microwave broccoli (a) until just tender. Drain and refresh under cold running water. Drain again and set aside.
3. Heat oil in a saucepan over a medium heat, add onion and cook, stirring, for 5 minutes or until onion is soft. Add garlic and basil (b) and cook for 3 minutes longer.
4. Place 90 g/3 oz tasty cheese (mature Cheddar), Parmesan cheese, cottage cheese and milk in a bowl and mix well. Add onion mixture, broccoli (c), pasta and black pepper to taste and mix to combine.
5. Transfer mixture to a lightly greased ovenproof dish, sprinkle with remaining tasty cheese (d) and bake at 240°C/475°F/Gas 9 for 15 minutes.
6. Place under a preheated hot grill and cook for 2-3 minutes or until top is golden.

Serves 4

tip from the chef

Other vegetables can be added to give color and texture –carrots, pumpkin, zucchini and mushrooms are all popular choices.

a

b

c

d

bean stew

◼☐ ☐ I Cooking time: 35 minutes - Preparation time: 15 minutes

method

1. Place beans in a large bowl, pour over enough cold water to cover and set aside to soak overnight, then drain. Place beans in a saucepan, pour over abundant cold water, bring to the boil over high heat. Reduce heat and simmer gently until beans are tender. Drain, set aside.

2. Heat oil in a frying pan over medium heat. Add red pepper, celery, carrots and onion and cook, stirring frequently, until vegetables are soft.

3. Add tomatoes and 2 cups/500 ml/16 fl oz water to pan, mix well and bring to the boil. Add beans and boil about 20 minutes.

Serves 4

ingredients

> **250 g/8 oz red dried beans**
> **100 g/3¹/₂ oz white dried beans**
> **5 tablespoons oil**
> **1 red pepper, cubed**
> **3 stalks celery, sliced**
> **2 carrots, sliced**
> **1 onion, chopped**
> **440 g/14 oz canned tomatoes, undrained and mashed**
> **freshly ground black pepper**

tip from the chef

For something different, use chickpeas in place of the beans and add one boneless chicken breast fillet, cut into cubes.

english
vegetable casserole

■☐☐ | Cooking time: 45 minutes - Preparation time: 15 minutes

ingredients

> 1 tablespoon oil
> 1 onion, chopped
> 2 tablespoons plain flour
> 2 cups canned tomatoes
> 1 cup tomato purée
> 1 tablespoon chopped fresh thyme
> 1/4 teaspoon black pepper
> 1 leek, sliced, white part only
> 4 spring onions, chopped
> 4 carrots, cut into thin strips
> 1 cup button mushrooms, sliced
> 3 stalks celery, sliced into thin strips

method

1. Heat oil in a large frying pan over a moderate heat and cook onion for 3 minutes. Sprinkle flour over onion and cook, stirring constantly for 2 minutes.
2. Add tomatoes, purée, thyme and pepper, cook for a further 5 minutes.
3. Add leeks, spring onions, carrots, mushrooms and celery, transfer casserole to an ovenproof dish, cover and cook in a moderate oven for 35 minutes. Garnish with fresh thyme sprigs if desired.

....
Serves 4

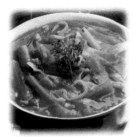

tip from the chef

This is an ideal main meal for vegetarians, but it can also be served as a side dish for all kinds of meat.

barley casserole

■ □ □ | Cooking time: 35 minutes - Preparation time: 10 minutes

method

1. Place barley in a large bowl, cover with water and set aside to soak for 2 hours. Drain well and set aside.

2. Heat oil in a large frying pan, add barley and cook over a medium heat, stirring constantly, for 10 minutes.

3. Add tomatoes, wine and tomato paste (purée) to pan, bring to simmering and simmer for 20 minutes. Add onion and cook for 5 minutes longer. Stir in olives and serve immediately.

ingredients

> **1 cup/200 g/6¹/2 oz barley**
> **2 tablespoons vegetable oil**
> **440 g/14 oz canned tomatoes, undrained and mashed**
> **¹/4 cup/60 ml/2 fl oz dry white wine**
> **3 tablespoons tomato paste (purée)**
> **1 large onion, chopped**
> **12 stuffed green olives, halved**

....

Serves 8

tip from the chef

Recent studies have shown that barley foods can lower cholesterol. Beta-glucan is thought to be the ingredient responsible for this. Beta-glucan is a type of fiber which blends with cholesterol and helps with its removal from the body. It is also found in oats, but not in wheat.

index

Introduction 3

Beef and Veal
Beef and Red Wine Casserole 16
Beef with Pumpkin & Lemon Grass 12
Crusty Steak and Kidney Pie 6
Olive and Meat Ragoût 10
Ossobuco.. 8
Paprika Beef 14
Seasoned Sausage Ragoût........................ 18

Lamb
Athenian Lamb Hotpot 26
Chunky Lamb Soup 20
Garlicky Lamb Pot Roast 28
Lamb Pot Roast 24
Lamb Stew with Lemon Sauce 22
Tomato and Thyme Shanks 30

Pork
Mustard Chilli Pork................................... 34
Tarragon Pork with Vegetables................... 32

Poultry
Chicken Biryani... 48
Chicken Cassoulet 38
Chicken Chasseur 36
Chicken with Chickpeas 40
Creamy Chicken with Sweet Potato 46
Duck with Ratatouille................................ 50
Farmhouse Casserole 42
Fruity Chicken Casserole 44

Rabbit
Marinated Rabbit Hotpot 52

Seafood
Baby Octopus in Red Wine........................ 54

Vegetables
Barley Casserole....................................... 62
Bean Stew 58
Broccoli and Macaroni Casserole 56
English Vegetable Casserole....................... 60